Butterfly

A

Rose

A Journey through

Transition

Butterfly

A

Rose

Emily Pittman Newberry

OneSpirit Press

Portland, Oregon

ISBN 1-893075-74-5
EAN 978-1-893075-74-0
LCCN: 2010937230

Cover Art and Design by Suzanne Deakins
Book Design Spirit Press

One Spirit Press
www. onespiritpress.com
onespiritpress@gmail.com
Portland, Oregon

My Mission

Out from the center
Of Spirit's amber sphere,
Finding the love
In smile or tear,
The changer is changing;
The future is here.

Dedication

To my brother Duncan, who washed his pain away with gin, and died leaving his children with bittersweet memories. Yet they carry on, bringing the best of him back to life.

As he lay dying I made a promise to turn my own pain and confusion into something positive, and here it is.

Beginning Words

I don't know whether life is harder to live or to tell. To live it is to be always improvising, even when you think you know the rules, because the rules start becoming irrelevant the moment something changes.

To write about life is hard because it's such an incredible journey, and so rich that no words can possibly capture what it was. That's one reason this came out as poetry, because right now I really don't have the words; and poetry for me right away forces the words to get beyond themselves.

That's what I'd like to do in life; be fully present and get beyond myself at the same time.

Emily Pittman Newberry

In The Beginning

Butterfly A Rose

"There is always a moment in childhood when the door opens and lets the future in."

Graham Greene

Butterfly A Rose

The Question 1

How do you live when
your dreams are more real than
the ground you stand on?

How do you sleep when
your nightmares follow you
like a shadow in the afternoon sun?

How do you walk when
your thoughts propel you
into alternate worlds where
emotions speak louder than words
and muddy is the main color?

I only wonder that I am still here
to tell the tale.

Death Creative

You can't live without
killing something every day;
just ask the corn, beans and chickens
who breathed their last
to fuel your next breath.

I used to eat in gulps
to bury my secret and
silence the whispers in my dreams.

What a shame to sacrifice a life
for the sake of a phony peace.
Sooner or later the secret will out
and all the brave stories will
slink away in shame.

Butterfly A Rose

The Last Time

When did my innocence
become hiding?

Was it the male sexed baby girl
who didn't demand dolls?

Was it the child retelling the story
of divorce denied that
left out the mother who
ran from her fear of conflict?

Was it the Boy Scout draped in proper
to hide from his "her"
he sheltered?

Was it the revolutionary shouting his shadow
and bludgeoning the gentle inside for a cause?

Was it the machinist, whose solid citizen routines
were the last bulwark
against the truth?

Or am I just asking about the past
to hold off the last onslaught
of vulnerability?

5

Yesterdays' Fears

My toes are at attention,
Sorry to mention,
The secret is out.
For every good deed
A maiden in need
Will cry and will pout.
But never forget,
Your heart will not let
You down.
Once I knew a boy
Bereft of joy,
Whose life was a toy
With chipped paint.
Bring me a tear
For yesterday's fear
Will soon be got out.

Butterfly A Rose

A Sterling Character

She was a sterling character,
earnest like a boy scout and
eager to please.
She took her cue from the
beatings and tongue lashings
that safety was in slumber
and tomorrow comes for
those who hide.

She got her Sterling name
before she even had a thought
of what to be.
It came with stories of perfection
and weighed down under
generations of expectations.

Butterfly A Rose

She accepted Sterling, a good lad,
he gave the right impression for awhile
until the pain caught up with him,
or the fear of being abandoned again
chased him from one home to another,
always searching for the one place
where they can't throw you out
or beat you into silence.

But Sterling was a cover
for she who thought to hide
behind a safe face.
She didn't even let him know
the score.
So on he went like his life was real,
until the weight of being an armor
was too much to hold.

Did he give up,
or did she?

A Sleeper

I walked so long asleep, in a nice
dream that didn't ask
any embarrassing questions,
that it was most
unsettling this morning
when a cold splash of
TV hit my mind.
It was the murmur of
distracted voices mirrored
in the lips mouthing nothing but
strange fears;

fears devoid of children's laughter;
no wonder I got disoriented.
Between my own sleepwalking
and the noise of yesterday is
no place for Grace.

Butterfly A Rose

A Weightless Heavy

I've gone in to the night
and come back with my
dreams in a knapsack
that, weightless as a result,
carried me into the heavens.
Yet what could be weightier
than a dream unfulfilled,
or a day without something
done that wasn't pre-planned?
Carry me again into your
deepest sleep and I will
promise to be faithful
to my heart.

The Show Must Go On

I didn't mean to go on forever,
it just happened that way,
one body of assumptions
flowing into the next;
it seemed rude to
interrupt the play I wrote
in the middle of a scene.

Should the lead just
announce her quandary as
she changed costume in the
middle of the stage?
I couldn't abide my own nakedness
so the play just went on.

Butterfly A Rose

My Body's Anger

My body rebelling;
nose running,
watery eyes itching,
sinus aching,
openly yelling
STOP!!!
Too much rich food,
sugar, salt, and flour,
taken in to soothe
the pain hour by hour;
maybe I can just
FEEEEEL!?!
Can I?

At The Abyss

Sometimes when I realize I've
gone years without writing a poem I just
want to cry.
What the hell is going on!?!?
Where are the hours I spent on
trivia going nowhere fast and
delving into nothing?

I sometimes feel like I'm
standing at the abyss
peering into the darkness
and often stepping away from the edge;
The forest and field behind me are so
inviting, why not linger there for a while
and keep my safe place in the world?

But something in me will not
stay put very long.
I get restless and feel impelled
to go over the edge.
But which one, and where?

Butterfly A Rose

Carry On Stranger

Carry on, stranger, for
the world is not your plan.
It's oysters you're after and
sleeping on dry land.
If ever after comes today,
you'll never know why you lost your way,
and the last thing ever you will say is
"Life on earth is grand!"
Then carry on, stranger,
your dream state for to keep.
You must not heed the music,
and do not look so deep.
The pleasant lies
might shock your eyes
revealing you're asleep.

A Slice of Life

Walking, weaving fictitious
stories in my mind;
fighting the demons
I create effortlessly,
as though they really inhabited my
waking world.
Suddenly I know,
I'm just praying:
"Dear God, help me make it through this day,
help me be closer to you.
Help me accept myself and
trust that there is love in this world."

Butterfly A Rose

I Don't Know

I don't know why
I let myself fall into
sadness or fear.
If not by chance as a raindrop
falls on a silent pond,
then by the design of a
careless heart
forgetting for a while
the danger that
awaits there.
Forever lost
would be my souls' story,
or taken in the embrace
of long forgotten gory
memories.

I Can't

"I can't!" So, you
finally said
out loud.
Busted for what
you are; the sad,
frightened child
cowering from the
blows, yes, but
more so from the fear
of their next falling.
The prisoner becomes
her own jailer.

No Time

I have no time
For myself,
I tell myself
And ask myself
Which "myself"
Is now in charge?
Time seems to fly
While doing stuff,
And while I stuff
That feeling stuff
I know that stuff
Is looming large.

Go where?

How many ways do
I hide?
And why?
Isn't a lifetime of
sorrow and blank
feelings enough?
If tears flow,
I will go
where?

My Sharp Words

I've gotten careless
with my words these days;
or haven't taken care enough
to think them through
my heart.

But that would soften the
edges of the knife
cutting through illusions
torn like yesterdays paper
in the birdcage where
my thoughts would be
imprisoned were it not
for the pouring out
of my soul.

What is My Name?

What is my name?
fool, naive one, or not
yet born to the truth?
I can't know the difference until
I stop eating gruel and
finally drink the
sweet nectar of nothing.

Living Long

Please help me God,
I can't contain
the sadness and
I can't let it out.
It leaks out and
weeps out and
still I hold
the line.
When is the end
of my time
of weeping?

But then I breathe
in reverent silence
and all is calm,
all is calm.
Sleep, the child,
who dreams of loving,
living long each
precious day.

When Did It?

When did rain become
a dreary note?
Only when sung as
autumns' bright leaves
turn brown and die,
floating to the ground
as if nothing mattered.

When did going home become
a sad thing?
Only in the winter
of my discontent;
when I forgot my friends,
shut out love
and played the victims' song.

Greetings cozy cave,
I fall into
your warm embrace,
smiling.

Butterfly A Rose

And, Sadly, I'm In Charge

I'm in danger of
losing the center
of my life.
Too many things
pulling this way and that.
Too many thoughts
saying what I can't do,
or I won't be accepted.
Too many distractions.
Yet, sadly, I
am in charge.

My Darkness

Darkness must be useful,
because there is
so much of it.
I have a deep well
and I reach into it
to face life.
But every time I go there
I seem to stir something deeper;
and it is wet, dark, and sad.
A bottomless well
of tears.

So Cold

So cold, so cold,
frosted windows, early meeting,
furiously scraping, slowly heating,
engine and warming body;

So cold, so bold
as to carry on
anyway.

So cold, so old
is the routine sleepwalk
between dream states,
writing my story
as if by automatic hand.

So cold, I'm told,
to keep the secret locked away,
so deep even my
own eyes were fooled
by the distance.

Where's the perspective in that?

Hope

I sit with quiet tears
washing away
the layers of protection.
as your soft voice
invites me to tremble
any way my body
needs to be.

I don't know if
I can even hope
for release from the pain?
Touch me and I'll touch you
as if eternity could sit
in a mason jar
preserving the perfect moment.

It takes heat,
and my heart has the gas to burn,
but something in the furnace
keeps blowing out the match.
It wouldn't do to illuminate
what's in that cellar.

Butterfly A Rose

Get Over It?

"Oh, get over it." I say to me,
But it isn't likely I'll bow down
to my own bossy self,
any more than
I ever did to others
who after all could only
control themselves.

The real question is, I think,
whether I will frustrate myself
enough to walk away from myself
as I have from others;
losing the intimacy
and the gifts
along with
the pain?

Another Choice

I am a wandering stream
flowing, twisting, winding down
from mountain to lowland sea.
And every place I long to stop
is not a place for me.
I'm made to dance
with rock and branch,
and flow through fishy gill.
And bubble, babble and run the rapids
going where they will.

But there's another choice I see;
to leave the stream and flow into
the thirsty ground
drunk up by the flowers
on the shore
to blossom, bloom, die
and be reborn
ever, ever more.

Butterfly A Rose

Lessons

Sorry, Mother, but I had to tell the truth,
though it was bitter at times
and the words catapulted
like they were escaping a too bright light.
You left and my child's heart
had no way to cry;
Father announced that it was time
to get on with the new life
and after all what would people say
when they discovered that the marriage ended.
Weren't children of divorce a problem
waiting to trouble the neighbors?

Sorry, Father, but I had to keep it all in
and hide my broken pieces before
someone swept them into the garbage.
I know I went off and picked them up,
putting them back together like a Picasso,
one piece out of alignment with the other.

Butterfly A Rose

What was well drawn in each small part,
looked awkward and disjointed
when viewed from afar.
Just so.

Sorry, Sterling, that I used you
to hide my nakedness
behind your idealism
and peeked out through your eyes
like a performer gauging the audience
before the play begins.
And there you were trying so hard
just to be on stage and saying your lines
like you meant every word.
And you did.
But my wanting to be out got in the way.

Sorry my dear Soul, for taking so long
to know that all my fears would get me
was loneliness
and a canyon wide gulf
between my dream of love
and the world of dreams
I was living.

Thank you, God, for this time
of learning about myself
and for keeping in touch
while I had my phone
on automatic forwarding
to the "out" file.

What Kind of Thanks is That?

What better escape than
long sweaty hours
married to axe and hammer and wedge?
Knotty elm fibers yield slowly
and muscles ripple in rhythm to
youthful blows.

Or yet the tractors' roar
as grass lies slain before it's blades,
and I, imagining I'm in control,
swing the beast round straight.

Better than the sneering words
landing on uncomprehending ears,
or the sharp tongue speaking in
leather belt shouts.

Thank you, Dad,
for the work
that saved my soul.

Butterfly A Rose

Lost and Found and
Lost Again

I lost you to angry words and
your fear of fighting.
What kind of mother would
think it best to disappear?
Was the marriage anger so deadly,
the barbs of a blind world so sharp,
that you saved me by your distance?

I found you again, showing up
with a sheepish grin
apologizing for my foolish questions.
We both agreed not to dive
too deep; we knew better.
You gave me what you could,
I gave you my sons,
at least I found a friend.

I lost you then
when the demons in your mind
dragged you to the
final dungeon and
locked the doors.
And I stood again
on the other side of lost
wondering what
I'd done wrong.

An Impenetrable Wall

You were introduced one day
as the new mother
to a baby's uncomprehending mind.
As the family grew larger
your demons grew angrier
and jumped out at just the right moments
to put scary into my memory banks.

You were good at cooking and
lashings of the tongue and belt,
and I took away a love of silence
that I held like a true belief
even when it cut through my life
and whipped my soul.

But we each got it right, finally;
You apologized and
I stopped the cycle of violence.
It's funny but I never felt closer to you
than the day you took back your dignity
by dying on your terms.
And taking your demons with you.

Butterfly A Rose

The Day The Music Died

It was a day
like any other,
filled with busy thoughts
and walking without much thought.
But somehow the trying too hard
to make success my goal,
became encrusted with
the trappings of him;
the nice guy I wore
like a shield or a business suit.

Somehow the trying built up
like a long forgotten volcano.
And the mountain wore down
from scraping against moon and stars.
With less weight and more pressure,
the woman exploded through my head
taking illusion on a scary ride
and leaving me wondering where
the script went.

The Journey

"When we are no longer able to change a situation, we are challenged to change ourselves." Victor Frankl

The Question 2

When I was a baby my dreams were reality,
the womb cast me forth and all was love.

When I was a child my reality became a dream;
I was torn from the womb and the world became
a movie made from different scripts
and a confusion of mothers.

When I was made a boy my reality became a nightmare,
and I tried to find a stable place to stand.
I only found it in my mind,
and could no longer feel my body.

When I became a man I was running
from stage to stage trying to find the right role,
but the lines never felt real.

When I broke through the thin veil,
peeled away the armor
and awoke from the dream,
I knew...
I was Emily.
The ground became solid,
the dream became real
and the answers woke up to
settle into the soft arms of
the next question.

The Graven Image

Isn't a graven image
something you worship
carved of wood or stone?
Then I lived 60 years as
my own graven image.
The man, wooden and frozen
to prevent the spontaneous woman
from popping out at
inopportune moments;
the worship of armor
surely strong enough
to keep away the
feared feminine spirit;
the incantations and prayers
to a false god desperately
invoked to ward off the nymph.
Ahh, release, and truth;
be my friend.

Butterfly A Rose

What Happened?

I was so lonely I
thought I'd been dropped
in the middle of nowhere
with a sitcom playing on
a wrap around TV.
You walked in and
turned your body and,
eyes away, hardly
noticing me until
two hours into the meal.
And I drank thankfully of
relief that I was in the room at all,
and stuffed my uncomfortable feelings with
a plunger made of mashed potatoes and chicken.
Later I came home and
found myself sinking, slowly
to the bottom of a cold, silent lake.
It was a lake I'd visited in
a waking dream long ago when
the weight of my father's image of me
joined with the paralysis of trying to be it
kept me on the bottom,

Butterfly A Rose

wondering whether I or the illusion
would die first.
And a long pole came down to
the bottom and pulled me out.
It was like that,
only this time I had
to pull myself out.
And everyone was trying
so hard not to notice
what's happened to me.

Lost In Paradise

I've tried being good, really,
and all I got was a mouthful of angry
of the permanent kind.
The whispers in my ears got louder
the more I shouted "No!"
And all my organs came together
to filibuster against
the very thought of it.

I wanted to cultivate kindness
and stabilize the dance with those I love.
But all the sweetness got me
was an empty heart
and a home echoing
what might have been.

Meanwhile the angels were laughing
and pointing to my separateness,
which I adopted before I knew
that stars don't shine through fog.

Butterfly A Rose

It Wasn't His Time

He's gone, the poor dear,
and the sounds of his
footsteps didn't register on
the pages of life.
Only once or twice
did someone know
his presence in a
way that was like touching
flowers gently.
Sure, he had a history, but
only the angels could
sit peacefully knowing
the sad truth of his
tortured nightmares.
Everyone else, including himself,
believed the whispers coming
from the soap opera written
in chalk on the sidewalk.
He skipped along, sometimes
even touching the lines,
which everyone knows will
break your mothers back.
Sleep little genie,
maybe the next universe will
be your stage.

I Don't Know Why

I don't know why
I let myself visit
the bottom of the lake.
It's not like I don't
notice when I've gone there.
The splash of cold water
in my body would
wake a sleeping bear.
Perhaps it seems safer
at the time than what
is happening on shore.
I run into some strangers
and the momentary
fragments of fleeting reactions
I thought I saw was
all I needed for an
excuse to go there.
And I think I'll choose again
not to drown this time.

Butterfly A Rose

Out of The Darkness

"Out of the darkness,"
said the muse,
"into the lightly
held moment. "
Even the dead have
no time anymore and
the living can't tell
if it's real.

Now While I'm Hot

Oh, how easy to forget,
the task that I set,
when the pattern's not the same.
I woke and added in
a walk in nature, and then
my mindless life became the game.
And somehow at the sink,
holding dirty dishes I think
one thought,
quickly caught,
I know I aught,
now while I'm hot,
to sit and write.
Ahhhhhhhh -- I breathe

Butterfly A Rose

I Wrote For So Long

The last time I wrote for this long
I danced in the streets of
my mind.
I was crazy, sure,
but that didn't blunt
the feeling of joy.
If I ever get around
to reading all this again,
I might relive the feeling
of God flowing through
my transparent body,
But somehow I always seem
to be too busy with nothing.

A Cup Of Sadness

I hold a cup of sadness,
while drinking deep of hope;
I teeter on the cliffs dark edge,
while climbing destiny's rope.
How can the truth be blurry,
when thinking seems so sure?
How can a cry of loneliness
be counted as a cure?
I only know the next thing
I pour into my cup
I'll drink in through my body
and wake the question up.

Butterfly A Rose

Of Struggling

The struggle to live my truth,
a gorgeous, fabulous truth,
that slaps the minds of those I love.
The struggle to stay
connected in love,
when others struggle
with good hearts
to be with me without
imposing their pain
or expressing their surprise.
Sometimes I just get
tired of struggling.

Surprise, Surprise

Surprise, surprise, sweet girl,
the breath you pull in and
push out doesn't have that
automatic glow you wanted.
It carries darker hues with it,
in and out, in and out;
did you think the dark
side would disappear
just because you
closed your eyes?
Meditate this, darlin',
what is, IS, in this moment.
Change won't come out
of unconsciousness.
Keep your eyes open or
risk surprise.

Butterfly A Rose

A Scratchy Message

I got a message
on bright white
paper.
The words were clear
but the message muddied up my eyes
as though the sound of the pencil
scratching across my ears
held the wrong colors,
or hadn't been sharpened
by rocks falling into cold streams;
That's okay,
they'll be rounded, if not soft,
In a few decades.

Holding Truth

Earthen jars were not meant
to hold molten metal,
any more than my earthy mind
can hold the light
of God's Truth.
One instant would melt me
into a lump of burnt offerings
to the little god of poor me
that I made up in a moment of
madness.

Lucky for me,
the one true God
that was revealed to me
in a mindless reverie
has infinite patience.

Surely it will take
the life of the universe
for my earthy mind
to take it all in.
Best to filter it
through my safe preconceptions.

Or I can just wait
until I finally cross over,
and merge with the blinding light
in a dance of pure joy.

I Got It Wrong

I got it wrong,
but only the wind could tell.
After it blew the leaves
into a pile of dust,
it went by me whooshing
like a train late for the
last station made of gold.

The next thing I knew
I held a poem
in the palm of my hand,
and the softness of its lines
forgave my transgression
on the rules I didn't want anyway.

Butterfly A Rose

You Have A Lot of Nerve

You have a lot of nerve
trying to be friendly
when I saw the startled look in your eye
the first moment we met.
Do you have any idea
how much energy I waste
trying not to be a bother
to you?
Sometimes I'm glad for
the respite of pretending
that nothing is going on.
But other times I just prefer
the possible pain of uncomfortable truth.
At least I know where I stand.
And do I dare hope
for transformation of us both?
I need the self acceptance
And you need, what???

An Easy Promise

I wish I could promise
to not change,
but the cells in my body keep dying,
leaving progeny in their wake.

Do you think I can make them
Be perfect copies
of those who came before?
When you figure out how,
let me know,
and I will go back
to what I was yesterday.

It's Okay, Little Darlin'

It's okay, little darlin'
To cry;
It's okay, little darlin'
To die.
The next moment awaits you
like a leaf greets the breeze;
the motion will freeze,
your fancy to please,
and laugh as you
come through the door.
So weep as it comes,
each tear falls so light;
and laugh for the hell of it
late in the night.
Your heart knows one thing,
it's easy to sing
if only you let yourself be.

It's Still Damn Hard

This isn't rocket science,
but it's still damn hard.

I know!
I agreed to come here
in this body,
and it isn't seemly to complain
But that's what I feel like anyway.

Only the lonely know
what I live each day,
and only the truly blessed
will take me away
from this crazy world.

Butterfly A Rose

It Drives Me Crazy

It drives me crazy!
I swear not to soldier on
but I do, I do.
It drives me crazy!
I will listen to my body,
but I don't, I don't.
It drives me crazy!
I need to go and cry,
but I won't, I won't.
It drives me crazy!

So The Story Goes

So the story goes, I said,
and my mind went blank.
Everything I know
I learned in the heat of battle,
or floating in heaven,
which I seldom do.
So the story goes, I said,
and my heart fairly sank
with the waiting for saviors
who laugh in your face
the moment you give your all.

So the story goes, I said,
with my belly like a tank
full of fears I ate
at yesterdays banquet.

So the story goes.

That is All

The Pain of loneliness
is unbearable but small,
compared to the waiting
for connection to all
that is.

And in my silent hour
when shoulders heave
and tears fall
on deaf walls;
I take one step
toward the doorway to freedom.
And that is all.

Butterfly A Rose

Smiling Fears

Meet me in the place
where your limbs crack
under the weight of
your fears.
We will brush them off
like soft dry snow,
and then melt them on the
ground with our
grateful tears.
Warmed like the sun,
drenched like the rain,
they smile the closer
we are to God.

Give Me Your Love

Give me your love and
I'll probably run like
crazy to some sad but
less scary cave.

I had a handle on this
love thing, or so I thought,
until I moved through the
curtain separating me from
myself, and found I changed.

I had a handle on this love thing,
but it wasn't solid enough
to carry me through
the change.

Give me your love,
and I'll probably run,
but only from the unknown
joy I cannot yet face.

Butterfly A Rose

The Channel

I've written eight days worth
this morning alone.
Alone, that is except for God
peering over my shoulder
smiling indulgently
like a father in love
with his sadly misled
but still lovable daughter.
I just need to reach back
and touch that gentle hand.
Then the spark of Truth
will run through me
like a current through a silver wire
and jump out to shock
whomever dares come close.

What I Would Do

Each letter I type
is another ghost
gone flying into the
unknown;
I can't retrieve it;
it has a life of
its' own now, and
I must play with it if
I want to touch it again.
Whose game is
making the rules, anyway?
Not mine, or I'd
surely make it dance to
my favorite tune.

Butterfly A Rose

Paying Attention

Ordinarily I wouldn't pay attention
to so small a thing
as the whisper of a breeze
when walking furiously
in the early morning light.

It wasn't the force of it
that got my attention,
and it didn't exactly grab me
or turn my head.

It was more like a gentle touch
that's so inviting
my attention couldn't not turn,
and turning be held softly
so I didn't turn away.

Awake! Awake!

Did I awake this morning?
Or did I just float
from one dream to another?
The heavy air of the room
only invited a few tears.
My shoulders burn
and the cleansing breath of God
sweeps away all
but the bare bones of weeping
revealed at last
as the early morning smiling mother
holding her child and whispering,
"Awake, awake, awake!"

Butterfly A Rose

Now What?

"In spite of the cost of living, it's still popular."
Kathy Norris

The Question 3

The joy of liberation runs through me
like a river past a broken dam.
All the years of holding back
could light a city with their power.
And they carry me like a fallen leaf
dragging bits of my life along
as I tumble blindly into
an ocean of possibility.

And what will I leave behind,
snagged on a branch or
caught behind a rock,
that I might long for and
never find again?
What will I run over in my
blind rush to freedom?

Butterfly A Rose

On Returning

Go down the mountain,
but don't run.
You'll miss the flowers along the way,
maybe even trample them,
and get a skinned knee
for your troubles.
For all the work it took
to reach the summit,
all the stumbles, falls
and scratched shins,
for all the exhilaration of
being at the top,
seeing forever,
being above the dark clouds
bathed in the brightest
sunlight there is,
much yet is to be missed
by hurrying on the way down.
The valley floor, after all,
will wait for you.

Butterfly A Rose

The North Star

Over the top of
the world a star
stands astride all
we hold dear.
"Cry if you must",
she says, "but
walk with me,
flowing down the
Milky Way, finding
a light 'neath every step."

After The Quandary, The Rent

This morning I
emailed my quandary.
It stared back as
though it didn't hear
my rumbling stomach or
see my faint smile.
Arguably, I haven't either
a rational basis for my thinking,
or a mystery to
my soul.
But then so what?
Arguably I'm not even here.
What's the fun in that?
I have grown
to like my confusion, thank you,
and to cherish the way I flitter about.
And now for the rent.

Butterfly A Rose

Sometimes It's Easier

Why do I have to be
torn into shreds like
the dead, dry autumn leaves
before waking all renewed?
It hurts!

Sometimes it's just easier
to give in to the chattering,
or externalize it with a
book or good web site
or TV or movie.
Sometimes, it's easier.

Passionate About Work

I like it when I feel
passionate about work;
even bone tired,
mind drained,
can't remember a name,
flip chart words
all look the same,
hung out to dry body;
I still like it when I feel
passionate about work.

Write Each Day

I write each day,
A word or two,
Maybe nothing to say,
Or what is said
Comes out like a
Flower from dung;
Not intended but
There any way.

Sometimes I Feel

Is it worth the pain?
The deep, searing
burning in the core
like I can't live
another day more
never will end pain?
But I am alive,
not subject to the endless cycle
of dead air followed by naive attempts
to finally live.
So much energy devoted
to keeping my inner woman
from coming out.
Intense energy
like an asbestos glove shielding me
from the inner fire.
Will it consume me,
or will it merely sacrifice
the old baggage into ashes
in service of a fuller life?
In the meantime,
trying to catch myself in the act
of medicating life away.

Butterfly A Rose

I Got It

I got it,
but didn't hold it
very well;
Soon it slipped away
into the laughter of bees
and the dancing of trees
and all the pretty little rocks.

If Love

If love grew
on every tree
it would only a fruit
of the season be.

If love oozed
from every pore,
it would be confined to body
ever more.

If love came
like rain from the sky,
with drying winds
would blow on by.

But love is essence
in all things;
expresses ground
of all beings.

Of the void
it shows all ways,
to be and never
end its' days.

Butterfly A Rose

Poor Cup

Poor cup, filled and emptied,
washed and rinsed and put away.
I never seem to appreciate you,
though I plainly love what you hold.
I use you as a vessel
for the gifts I give myself each morning.
My hands grip the handle
but I can't hold a candle
to your quiet giving way.

Can I Not?

What goes into being tired?
The every day living
of this body;
the thinking and doing
of work and play;
holding the fear of not being accepted;
working to blend in.

So, why not reduce
my own contribution?
Would I then be less tired?
Can I walk without fear,
be just as I am
without the burden
of protecting others
from their own fears?
Can I not?

Butterfly A Rose

For Tune Ate

Fort, the walls I build to keep
Myself asleep.
For Tu, my beloved, I sing;
Four tunes tickling my minds ear,
For tune, I like the melody I hear;
Fortune, a look into the future;
Fortune, a heap of dough;
Fortunate to be alive;
Fortunately it doesn't matter.

Ah, Progress!

The day is not yet here
and already I am
living it vividly
in my mind.
But fortunately less
than other times
just before the crack of dawn,
when I lived through weeks
at a time.
Ahh, progress!

Butterfly A Rose

My Exquisite Mind

It keeps me running,
so keep your hands off
my exquisite mind.
Only a fool would let go
of what served them so well, so long.
But then, so long
for repetitive thoughts
and repeating victories,
mindless scores against
ephemeral enemies;
Come home, darlin',
the tea is hot
and sweet.

I Worked So Hard To Get Here

I worked so hard to get here,
why am I hesitating
to stop and luxuriate
in the mountain meadow,
filled with the flowers
I planted for so many moons
again and again?

This is what I dreamed of,
and yet, I stumble on
as if the destination
was far off.

Butterfly A Rose

Like I Really Mean It

I am so lost in the morning
when I haven't time to prepare
or plan.
So what's the story
I tell myself?
I really don't want to tell it now,
because I'm trying to let it go.
What's that in my heart?
A touch of shame, perhaps?
And sadness mixed with fear?
I've so much to be grateful for,
and friends to see today.
let it all come to me.
Come and I will flow through it
Like I really mean it.

My Little Cave

Do I dare invite friends into my home?
It's like a cave with a rock or crevice
for every part of my inner life.
Like me it has strong outer walls,
and inside, the thing I'm captured by
leaks over onto the piles of stuff
I've put aside, for now.
And when I'm done with that,
I'll tidy up a bit,
or very sometimes, worry a lot,
And wander among the piles
until something else
blossoms for a while.
It's safe for now
from prying eyes and tut-tut thoughts
sneaking in with friendly eyes
looking and hiding what's behind;
or so I tell myself
and shut out what imagination conjures
out of nothing.

Butterfly A Rose

One More Time

There is no sadness like
a missed promise
or the ending of summer
in my heart.
The promise will remain
and summer will return,
and I will rise
to write again
one more time.

Getting Better

I got better at something yesterday.
It wasn't something I sought out
like the latest cool workshop,
or the ability to play
in a rock band.
Yet somehow I feel more like smiling
because I caught myself making angry sounds,
typing furiously as if the keys would shoot down my fears
with machine gun precision if only I typed fast enough
to not notice the feeling flowing through my fingers.
I got better at something
and it smelled of daffodils or baby skin,
creeping up on me
before I knew
what I was doing.

The Morning After

The morning after
I woke from a dream,
the sun rose as always
and kissed the earth as though
for the first time.

The morning after
I walked away
from the nest,
I fell into the arms
of a safety
that never ends
its vigil.

The morning after
I changed my body
I looked in awe
to find myself
in untouched form.

The morning after
I fell into his arms
I only knew the barest vowels
of the first words
in the next question.

The First Morning

Isn't this the first morning
when the first sun rose
to wash my childish face?
Isn't this the first time
I sat, still, in this place?
Isn't this the first line
that spoke to me of grace?
Take me, wake me, shake me;
sing the first song,
while the memory of ecstasy
carries me on.

Butterfly A Rose

The Ducks

I like to walk around the pond
watching the ducks dance
to the rhythms of a tune
I cannot hear.
I only see the steps and hear their calls
as the music rises and falls.

Now a pair swooping in, sliding to a stop
like a water skier coming to shore.
Then perhaps a round of loud quacking
followed by a flourish of wings
shaking away some energy or tension
in the soul.

Then again a quiet swim
with ducklings swirling around
like a chorus
of out of tune violins
that somehow manage
to end on the same note.

Don't worry,
I'll be back even if I am
deaf to the song.

Hope Came In The Window

Hope came in the window last night,
like a breath of fresh air
wrapping itself around my self doubt and
taking my bad dreams on a quiet walk to yesterday;
a lonely street where the old lines
are whispered by forgotten actors
trying once again to be called to the real stage.
But hope has its own plot,
and I signed up for the whole season,
in a role I'm going to write
one day at a time.

Butterfly A Rose

Just Another Angel

So what did you think was
going to happen
When you dropped your soul
into the abyss?
Only angels or fools
put blind faith in flying,
and you sure don't have wings.
At least now you know
this is only an illusion,
and really you are,
underneath it all,
just another angel.

Emily Pittman Newberry is an organizational development consultant, poet and child of God somewhat less confused than before she woke up one more time. In her personal life she tries to be present in between all the doing. In her professional life she works with teams to transform how they talk about difficult subjects. Her web site is www.wizense.com.

Emily does readings and is available for speaking engagements. Keep up with her current schedule at www.butterflyarose.com. To schedule a reading or speaking engagement, email Emily at butterflyarose@gmail.com.

Butterfly A Rose

Colophon

Text set in Garamond

Titles Bickham Script Pro

using Adobe Indesign

Printed in USA

onespiritpress.com
onespiritpress@gmail.com

Fini

8156295R0